TEX-MEX FROM SCRATCH

PAVILION

BY: Jonas Cramby
PHOTOGRAPHY BY: Roland Persson

CONTENTS

Left: Beef chilli taco (p.70)

FOREWORD

TEX-MEX FROM SCRATCH

My name is Jonas Cramby and I'm addicted to tacos. I love Tex-Mex food so much that I named my eldest daughter Dixie as her first name and Margarita as her middle name, and my youngest daughter Lone Star (after the nickname for the state of Texas). And if I ever have a third, she'll be named Carnita – after my favourite taco filling (recipe on p.78).

And just to make things clear here, we're not talking about that kind of horrible ready-made Mex that national league football players like, neither are we talking about bordering-on-racist Tex-Mex parties with Tequila Slammers, fake moustaches and 'funny' sombreros, or Friday nights in with hard taco shells that break up and fall all over your knee after the first bite. But about really tasty, homemade Tex-Mex grub made from scratch.

Because even though the word 'Tex-Mex' has carried a negative connotation for a long time, it's about as intelligent to reject a whole cuisine on these grounds as to say they have bad food in Italy because you can also get spaghetti bolognese in a jar.

Real Tex-Mex is actually, like so many other good things, the result of a culture clash. German immigrants brought their smoky sausages and creamy potato salads to Texas, and these food traditions were soon merged with the cowboys' simple prairie grub and the Mexicans' beautiful food culture – which in turn was a fusion between the Spanish and American Indian cuisines. The result became simple food that is easy to like and that makes you happy.

This more and more people seem to begin to understand. The word 'taco' is nowadays the most frequent search term on recipe sites, and in the US the Mex-grub is currently experiencing a revival. Many of the country's hip young restaurateurs have left their restaurants to start mobile food places in so-called taco trucks. The Mex-inspiration is also noticeable in American fine dining with the chef Rick Bayless in the forefront, and in Texas the

LUCK

long-despised Tex-Mex cuisine, eagerly egged on by the food journalist Robb Walsh, has become re-evaluated and is now seen as a proud part of the state's cultural heritage.

And it's from the states bordering Mexico in general, and from Texas in particular, that I have gathered inspiration for this cookbook.

It all began about 12 years ago when I went for my first road trip through the US. When I reached the states on the border to Mexico, I soon started to take notice of all the small, ramshackle street-food joints and rusty taco trucks, which had colourful signs boldly stating that here I would find tacos ricos (delicious tacos), tacos los mejores del mundo (the best tacos in the world) or tacos super-fantasticos (as it sounds).

That such good food could be cooked in hovels felt a bit like bragging to me. But the thing was, it was true, almost all these places actually served the world's best Tex-Mex grub. For only a few pounds I could get a pile of mesquite-grilled meat, served in a soft, warm home-baked wheat tortilla with grilled salad, onion and a couple of big crispy radishes on top – then a twist of lime and a big spoonful of smoky hot homemade salsa to finish it off. Or why not carnitas? Slow cooked, sweet-spicy pork with a small bowl on the side filled with the frying juices for dipping. Or a plateful of barbecued pork or beef: smoky, tender and sticky, served on a piece of paper with only a couple of crackers and a Mexican beer, so cold that your front teeth could almost crack.

'Tex-Mex is simple food that is easy to like and that makes you happy.'

When I came back home, I missed these places, like you miss an old friend. So I soon made sure that more and more work trips and holidays took me to the states bordering Mexico, and after a while I also started to put my head into the kitchens and ask for the recipes. When I returned home, I started to experiment, refine and adjust the cooking processes to my home conditions and realised that you actually could, with a minimal amount of effort, cook the world's best everyday food at home.

In this book, I will teach you just that. I will go through the basics as well as the more advanced. I will gather inspiration from both sides of the border, and it will include parts from each section of the Tex-Mex cuisine's food circle – crispy, hot, sweet, sour and sticky. But above all, it will be super-fantastico.

– Jonas Cramby

PART 1

BASICS

The first thing you need to know about cooking Tex-Mex food is that it's fun and colourful with a huge amount of flavour. So be generous with the lime and the chilli. The second thing is: no cans, jars or plastic packages can be used. Here we do everything from scratch.

Tortilla Press
Tortilladora

Tortillas

RECIPE OVERLEAF

TORTILLAS AND BURGER BUNS

If you want to start making your own tortilla bread, you need to know that there are two different kinds: wheat and corn. The Mexican corn tortilla tastes delicious and, well, corny – but only in its literal sense – while the wheat tortilla is a bit smoother, breadier and softer. The wheat variety is also the classic Tex-Mex tortilla and is used for tacos and when larger bread is needed, for example when making enchiladas and burritos.

Homemade wheat tortillas

If you absolutely have to, I can consent to using ready-made tortillas that you heat up in the oven. They are okay. But if you really want to impress, you should of course make your own. It's a lot easier than you think.

About 16 large (20cm/8in)
or 30 small (10cm/4in)

1.4kg/3lb/10 cups plain (all-purpose) flour
1 tsp baking powder
1 tsp salt
50g/2oz/4 tbsp butter
600ml/1 pint/2½ cups warm water

Mix the dry ingredients together. Dice the butter into small cubes and add to the flour mix. Slowly pour over the warm water. Mix together to a sticky dough. Knead on a floured worktop for about 2 minutes, put it back into the bowl and cover with damp kitchen paper. Leave to rest for 20 minutes. Once the dough has rested, divide into 16 or 30 portions and roll into small balls. Roll out the balls to round tortilla breads. Leave to rest for 10 minutes. Fry the breads in a dry frying pan for about 30 seconds on each side and serve them *à la minute* if you want to be fancy. Alternatively, preheat the oven to 100°C/212°F/Gas mark ¼, and then reheat them just before serving, preferably wrapped in a towel or in a tortilla warmer. If you'd like those fancy grill stripes, you can also fry them in a griddle.

Homemade corn tortillas

Corn tortillas are a bit trickier than the wheat variety – but also tastier if you get it right. Remember they have to be eaten straight away. Wheat tortillas you can prepare a couple of hours in advance and then reheat, while corn tortillas start tasting like Play-Doh after only half an hour. Although day-old corn tortillas are the ones to use if you want to make your own nachos, crispy tacos or tostadas. Just deep-fry, drain on a piece of kitchen paper and season with salt. Delicious! You do, however, need some special equipment:

MASA HARINA (CORN FLOUR)

Masa harina is a corn flour made from corn kernels that have been treated with slaked lime before being ground. To use, just mix with water and salt. It cannot be replaced by ordinary cornflour (cornstarch) or anything else – the only alternative in that case is to produce your own masa harina, but then you need Maíz Pozolero and slaked lime, so let's not bother right now. The most common masa harina brand over here is called Maseca and can be found in most Latin American food shops, speciality delis or can be ordered online.

TORTILLA PRESS

Since the dough made with masa harina is delicate and crumbly, you need a tortilla press if you want to make your own corn tortillas. If you do have one of these, however, it's very easy (and fun). You can either make your own tortilla press, buy one in a shop or online.

TORTILLA WARMER

Can be replaced with tea towels, but if you take your Mex-food seriously, you'll get a much better result with a proper tortilla warmer. The corn tortilla softens perfectly and will keep warm for hours. Can be ordered online or from a mate visiting the US.

Once you've got all the equipment, it's easy. Just mix the flour with water and salt according to the instructions on the packet, mix to a dough and roll into equally sized balls. Place some damp kitchen paper on top so that the balls don't dry out. Place the ball in the tortilla press – which you'll have covered in clingfilm (plastic wrap) or a plastic bag so that the dough doesn't get stuck – and press down. Be assertive, but don't go nuts and whack it like it's a theme park attraction. Lift up the press and, *voilà*!, there it is. Your very first corn tortilla. Remember that the rounder you make the ball, the rounder the tortilla will be. Fry your tortillas in a dry medium-warm Teflon frying pan. When they're done they are hard and don't seem very tasty at all. That's when you put them into your tortilla warmer, where they keep warm for ages and turn nice and soft.

Homemade tortilla crisps

I promise, once you've started making your own tortilla crisps you will never eat those sad excuses you can buy from the shop again. There's just one problem: you have to make them from real corn tortillas – preferably ready-made ones from a Latin American food shop, speciality deli, restaurant or ordered online – no worries if they're dry, the result will only be better if they are. The reason for making the crisps using ready-made tortillas is because those you make yourself won't be thin enough to achieve maximum crispiness. And you should absolutely not use wheat tortillas, it won't just turn them less nice, it will become outright inedible.

real corn tortillas
oil, for deep-frying
salt

Heat the oil to about 180°C/350°F and slice the tortilla into quarters. Deep-fry a couple at a time until golden yellow but not brown, and drain on a piece of kitchen paper. Season with salt and serve with guacamole or a homemade salsa.

Homemade burger buns

An extremely fluffy and soft bun that at the same time can stand up to some meat juice is crucial for a tasty hamburger. Today there is simply no commercial burger bun that ticks all the boxes. But how about bread from the bakers? Well, most of them are too wrapped up in their world of flavour-rich sourdough bread with a good crust to realise that some bread should neither taste too much nor offer too much chewiness.

About 12 buns
50ml/2fl oz/¼ cup instant potato mash powder
300ml/10fl oz/1¼ cups milk
20g/¾oz fresh yeast
2 tbsp granulated sugar
1 tsp salt
600g/1¼lb/4¼ cups strong wheat flour that makes the bread extra fluffy
1 egg
50g/2oz/4 tbsp butter, melted

Bring 200ml/7fl oz/generous ¾ cup water to the boil and whisk in the instant mash powder. Heat the milk to 37°C/98.6°F, crumble the yeast into a bowl, add the milk and stir until the yeast has dissolved. Add the sugar, salt and instant mash, and stir. Add the flour and work the dough in a food processor until smooth. Add the egg and mix a little longer. Pour over the melted butter and continue to work the dough until you have a smooth, fairly loose dough. Leave to rise for 1 hour. With damp hands, shape the dough into 12 round buns and place on a piece of baking parchment. Leave to rise for 1 hour without covering.

Preheat the oven to 200°C/400°F/Gas mark 6. When the buns have proved, spray with water, place in the oven with a dish filled with water underneath and bake for about 15 minutes or until they've turned a good colour. Take the buns out of the oven, spray them with water again and cover with a tea towel. Once cooled, remove from the baking parchment, put them in a plastic bag and seal. This will make the buns go even softer. While you're at it, take the opportunity to make a large batch; they're perfect for freezing.

Brioche-style burger buns

American fine-dining burgers are often served in a brioche bun.

About 8 buns
250ml/9fl oz/generous 1 cup tepid water
3 tbsp tepid milk
2 tsp dried yeast
2½tbsp granulated sugar
2 large eggs
750g/1lb 10oz/3⅓ cups plain (all-purpose) flour
2½ tbsp butter
1½ tsp salt
sesame seeds (optional)

Mix together the water, milk, yeast and sugar. Leave to stand for 10 minutes. Meanwhile, whisk 1 egg until it gets fluffy. In a large bowl, mix the flour and butter with your hands, as you would do with a shortcrust pastry dough. Stir in the yeast mixture, salt and the whisked egg until a dough appears as if by magic. This dough you will then knead – either by hand or in a food processor – about 8–10 minutes. It will be a bit stickier than a normal dough but that's okay. Shape into a ball, cover with a tea towel and leave to rise for 1–2 hours. Divide the ball into 8 portions that you roll into small, round, fine balls. Place on a baking tray lined with baking parchment and leave to rise under the towel for another 1–2 hours.

Preheat the oven to 200°C/400°F/Gas mark 6, and place a dish filled with water at the bottom. Whisk the other egg together with 1 teaspoon of water and brush over the buns. If you'd like a darker colour, like in the picture, you can also try adding 1–2 teaspoons bicarbonate of soda (baking soda). Sprinkle over the sesame seeds (if you want) and bake until the buns are golden brown, about 15 minutes. Leave to cool for a moment before gobbling them all up. It's difficult, but in one way or another it has to work.

GUACAMOLE

Guacamole makes you happy, and that's that. It's hard to think about diseases, ageing and death if you have a frosty mango margarita in your hand and a bowl of newly fried tortilla crisps and some guacamole on the table. So don't cheat with half-made stuff and hand mixers, do it from scratch.

Chunky guacamole

This guacamole should be chunky, so you absolutely may not put the avocado in a blender, if you do you're just lazy and might just as well go out and buy a take away.

Serves 4

8 avocados
4 tbsp freshly squeezed lime juice
2 tbsp salt
4–6 garlic cloves, chopped
1 small bunch of fresh coriander (cilantro)
4 fresh red or green chillies, e.g. jalapeño or medium-hot chillies
150ml/5fl oz/$^2/_3$ cup pico de gallo (see p.26)

Mash the avocados using a pestle and mortar. Add the lime juice, salt, chopped garlic, coriander and chillies. Taste and adjust the seasoning if needed. Then add a little bit of the pico de gallo and taste again, with the help of a tortilla crisp. If you are unsure about how much of each ingredient to use, note that the heat from the chilli should be balanced with the acidity of the lime and the saltiness of the salt.

Guacamole tipico

This Mexican everyday 'guaca' is more similar to an avocado salad than to the green cream that we associate to when hearing the word 'guacamole'. The trick is to get the chilli paste to cover every little bit of the avocado so that it's hot and salty at first and then smooth and soft.

Serves 2

2 tsp finely chopped white onion
1 tbsp finely chopped fresh chilli, e.g. jalapeño or red/green chilli
1 tbsp finely chopped garlic
$^1/_2$ tsp salt
200g/7oz/4 cups fresh coriander (cilantro)
2 avocados
1–2 tbsp freshly squeezed lime juice

Mash the onion, chilli, garlic, salt and half of the coriander to a fine paste using a pestle and mortar. Dice the avocados, squeeze over some lime juice, and stir into the mashed dressing so that all pieces are covered. Garnish with the rest of the coriander.

How much?

If you are unsure about how much guacamole to make, it's better to do too much than too little. One in fact cannot make too much guacamole. It has never happened.

Guacamole con piña y pepino

This fruity and crunchy 'guaca'-variation goes perfectly together with all types of barbecue.

Serves 4

1 cucumber
½ red onion
½–1 fresh habanero chilli
2 tbsp freshly squeezed lime juice
1 tsp salt
4 avocados
½ fresh pineapple
1 small bunch of fresh coriander (cilantro)

Peel and dice the cucumber, finely chop the onion, mash the chilli and mix everything together with lime juice and salt. Dice the avocados and fold into the mixture. Dice the pineapple, chop the coriander and add just before serving.

Taco shop guacamole

The exception that proves the rule: now it's okay to put the avocado in a blender. The purpose is not to save time however, but to create a smooth sauce for tacos and barbecued meat, that is made even creamier with a little crème fraîche.

Serves 4

3 green or yellow tomatoes (not red ones)
4 tomatillos
3 garlic cloves
3 fresh green chillies, e.g. medium-hot chillies or jalapeños
1 tsp salt
1 small bunch of fresh coriander (cilantro)
3 avocados
200ml/7fl oz/generous ¾ cup crème fraîche

Boil the tomatoes, tomatillos, garlic and salt without water (the tomatoes contribute with the liquid) for about 15 minutes. Leave to cool. Mix in a blender with coriander and avocados until you have a smooth sauce. Add the crème fraîche.

Guacamole con manzana

Over-18s-only 'guaca' with apple, tequila and pecan nuts might sound a bit weird but it tastes great. Promise.

Serves 2

1 green apple
1 tbsp tequila
1 tbsp freshly squeezed lime juice
1 fresh green chilli, eg medium-hot chillies or jalapeños
1 tsp salt
½ white onion
100g/3½oz/⅔ cup pecan nuts
2 avocados
fresh coriander (cilantro)

Peel and dice the apple and mix together with tequila and lime juice. Toast the chillies in a dry pan and mash together with the salt and onion using a pestle and mortar. Toast the nuts in the same pan. Dice the avocados, stir in the coriander and mix everything together.

About tomatillos

Tomatillo is a sour fruit that tastes like a cross between a physalis or Cape gooseberry and a tomato. It can be found in jars in South American food stores, speciality delis or fresh at good greengrocers. If you can't find any, you can replace them with physalis – even though you won't get the same green colour.

1.
2.
3.
4.
5.
6.
7.
8.
9.

CHILLIES AND SPICES

Chillies, dried and fresh, are an important part of the Tex-Mex cuisine, and in this day and age, there are so many varieties that it's easy to get confused. Here is a short introduction to the most common varieties.

1 Jalapeño

Green little fatties that are becoming more and more common in supermarkets, they have a more consistent heat than ordinary chillies, so do choose jalapeños if you can get hold of them. The darker the green, the hotter the chilli.

2 Guajillo

This fruity, mild chilli is perfect for all kinds of pork or for salads.

3 Chile piquin

When you eat street food in Mexico, you often get a couple of these little mini chillies on your plate together with a wedge of lime. The idea is that you should be able to control the heat and the acidity yourself.

4 Spice mixes

Make a large batch of these spice mixes and store in the cupboard then you're always ready if you fancy ribs or pulled pork or something. Here are a couple that are used often.

RENDEZ-VOUS DRY RUB

This useful spice mix, invented at the classic rib restaurant Rendez-vous in Memphis, is a perfect match for both pork and chicken.

8 tbsp paprika
4 tbsp garlic powder
4 tbsp chilli powder
3 tbsp ground black pepper
3 tbsp salt
2 tbsp whole celery or fennel seeds
1 tbsp crushed celery or fennel seeds
4 tsp yellow mustard seeds
1 tbsp dried oregano
1 tbsp dried thyme
1 tbsp whole coriander seeds
1 tbsp crushed coriander seeds
1 tbsp Knorr Aromat Seasoning

Mix together the dry rub in a bowl. Stored airtight it will last a long time.

FUEGO SPICE MIX

If you'd like an all-round spice mix, easy to hand in the cupboard, this one is perfect. Can be used for everything grilled or fried, even vegetables. Can also be used to flavour your tortilla crisps or popcorn.

3 tbsp paprika
1 tsp cayenne pepper
1 tsp ground white pepper
1 tbsp freshly ground black pepper
1 tbsp garlic powder
1 tbsp chilli powder
1 tbsp dried oregano
1 tbsp salt

Mix the spices together and store in an airtight jar.

BARBECUE RUB

When slow-cooking meat in a barbecue smoker strive for a 'bark' coating. The bark is the hard, caramelised coating that locks in juices and adds flavour.

100g/3½ oz/½ cup demerara (raw brown) sugar
100g/3½oz/½ cup granulated sugar
5 tbsp paprika
1½ tbsp salt
1½ tbsp garlic powder
1 tbsp freshly ground black pepper
1 tbsp ground ginger
1 tbsp onion powder
1 tsp dried rosemary

Mix the sugars and spices together and store in an airtight jar.

5 Habanero

Fruity and more spicy than the other fresh chillies. Use with caution. Perfect for fruity salsas.

6 Chipotle

A dried and smoked jalapeño, which is a must if you are making chilli. Boil or toast before making into a purée. It will add a deep, smoky flavour to your food. Often sold in packs together with ancho chillies.

7 Ancho

Dried chilli that you boil or toast and then make into a purée – used in salsas or stews for an unbeatable depth in flavour. Often sold in packs together with chipotle.

8 Chile de arbol

A classic dried chilli. To use, crumble with your fingers and sprinkle over food that's far too bland.

9 Red/green chilli

The most common chilli in supermarkets, it can be yellow, green or red and vary a lot in heat. So do taste before you pop it into the stew.

10 Poblano

The poblano pepper looks like a large chilli and tastes like a mix between a bell pepper and a jalapeño. If you can't get hold of fresh poblano, you can replace it with pointed peppers together with a chilli for extra bite.

A few words on cheese

Mexican cheeses are frequently used in the American states over the border, but can unfortunately be a bit more difficult to source in the UK. However, the good news is, you can replace them. **Queso fresco** is, for example, used for crumbling over tacos but can be replaced with a mild feta cheese. **Quesillo** is a soft, stringy cheese, perfect for using on quesadillas and taquitos, that can be replaced with mozzarella. **Requesón** is a mild, spreadable fresh cheese used for enchiladas, that much resembles ricotta. And the originally Spanish, yellow **Manchego** cheese you can also get hold of over here and is always prepared to step in whenever cheese is required.

10.

SALSA AND STUFF

To compare homemade salsa with a shop bought version is like comparing a three-course dinner in a fancy restaurant with eating spaghetti hoops straight from the can while watching a reality show. The salsa is the hot beating heart in Tex-Mex cooking, so take it seriously.

Salsa roja

The classic red salsa that, together with salsa verde, in some states is almost used in the same way as salt and pepper.

Serves 4

1 ordinary onion
4 tomatoes
6 garlic cloves
4 dried chillies, e.g. ancho or guajillo
100–200ml/3½–7fl oz/scant ½–generous ¾ cup chicken stock (broth)
1 small bunch of fresh coriander (cilantro)
salt

Cut the onion and tomatoes into quarters and boil together with the garlic and the deseeded dried chillies in so much stock that they're just covered, for about 15 minutes. Leave to cool. Mix everything in a blender together with the coriander and strain through a sieve so that the skin and seeds disappear. Season to taste.

Salsa verde

This lovely salsa uses tomatillos to get its green colour and sweet-sour taste (see p.18), but if you can't find it you can replace it with physalis or Cape gooseberries.

Serves 4

6 tomatillos
1 white onion
3 garlic cloves
1–2 fresh chillies, e.g. jalapeños
1 small bunch of fresh coriander (cilantro)
2 tbsp corn oil
salt

Roast the tomatillos, white onion, garlic and jalapeños in the oven on a high temperature until golden. Blend to a smooth salsa. Add the coriander and blend for a little longer. Heat the oil in a pan, add the salsa, and reduce until nice and thick. Season with salt. Leave to cool.

Salsa cocida

A fresher, little less hot, smooth everyday salsa that is quick to prepare.

Serves 4

200g/7oz cherry tomatoes
1 ordinary onion
6 garlic cloves
2–3 fresh red chillies
1 small bunch of fresh coriander (cilantro)
salt

Preheat the oven to maximum. Cut the tomatoes and onion into quarters and roast together with the garlic and the deseeded chillies in the oven until charred. Leave to cool. Mix in a blender together with the coriander. Season to taste.

Pico de gallo

'Pico de gallo' means the beak of the rooster and that's how a perfect pico should taste – like little chilli-hot rooster pecks on the tongue.

Serves 4

200g/7oz cherry tomatoes
1 white onion
1 small bunch of fresh coriander (cilantro)
1–2 fresh chillies
2 tbsp freshly squeezed lime juice
1 tsp salt

Halve the tomatoes and remove the seeds. Chop together with the onion, coriander and chillies, the finer the better. And if you don't like coriander, use it anyway. It's time you give up such silliness. Squeeze over the lime and season with salt. The flavour combination of lime and salt is the linchpin of Mexican cuisine, and it's crucial you get it right. It should be acidic enough to get your mouth watering but salty enough to balance this.

Mango salsa

This sweet-spicy, fruity salsa goes well with fish, shellfish and pork – and is perfect for carnitas. Habanero is awfully hot, so be careful, especially if you're a bloke and you all of a sudden need to go for a wee...

Serves 4

2 mangos
½ red onion
1 small bunch of fresh coriander (cilantro)
1–2 tbsp freshly squeezed lime juice
½–1 fresh habanero chilli
½ tsp salt

Finely chop the ingredients and mix together in a bowl. Serve cold.

Salsa para mariscos

This classic, green salsa is perfect for shellfish and fish. Fresh.

Serves 4

1 cucumber
4 large ripe tomatoes
1 white onion
2 fresh chillies, e.g. medium-hot chillies or jalapeño
fresh coriander (cilantro), to taste
2 tsp salt (which might sound like a lot but that's that)

Peel and deseed the cucumber. Finely chop the cucumber and tomatoes and place in a bowl. Then finely chop the onion, chillies and coriander, and add to the cucumber. Add the salt and stir together a little.

Green herby salsa

Beautifully green and fruity from the olive oil. Not a salsa for dipping but perfect for ceviche.

Serves 4

2 garlic cloves, skin left on
1–2 fresh green chillies, e.g. medium-hot chillies or jalapeño
2 tbsp olive oil
1 large bunch of fresh coriander (cilantro)
1 bunch of fresh parsley
1 cucumber
2 avocados
salt

Toast the garlic and chillies in a dry frying pan. When they've turned a nice colour, peel the garlic, deseed the chillies and mix together with the oil and the herbs in a blender. Peel and deseed the cucumber and chop into neat quarters. Do the same for the avocado. Season to taste.

Pickles
RECIPE OVERLEAF

PICKLES

Pickled vegetables are a bit like a crispy ketchup – with only a few easy trimmings you immediately increase the acidity, sweetness and crunch in a dish. All of the following recipes (except perhaps the eggs) go well together with tacos and barbecue.

Pickled red onion

Pickled red onion is a Mex classic which works with pretty much all types of tacos and grilled meat. Add some beetroot brine if you want to intensify the red colour.

Serves 4

2 red onions
200ml/7fl oz/generous 3/4 cup white wine vinegar
50g/2oz/1/4 cup granulated sugar
1 tbsp salt
1 bay leaf
1/2–1 fresh chilli, e.g. habanero
1 tbsp beetroot brine (optional)

Thinly slice the onions. Mix all the other ingredients together in a pan and bring to the boil. Add the onions and simmer for 30 seconds. Leave to cool and transfer to a nice jar together with the chilli. Leave in the fridge for 6–8 hours until the onion slowly changes colour from red-white to a beautiful light pink. Will keep for a couple of days in the fridge.

Quick pickled carrots

If you can't garner the time or effort to start pickling several days in advance, you can try this quick version of pickled carrots.

1 jar

2 carrots
2 garlic cloves
1–2 fresh red or green chillies, e.g. medium-hot chillies or jalapeño
100ml/3½fl oz/scant 1/2 cup white wine vinegar
1 tsp salt
1 tsp granulated sugar
1 bay leaf
5 whole white peppercorns

Cut the carrots nice and evenly into long thin strips, like matches, so-called julienne (Google it!). Slice the garlic and chillies (keep the seeds) and mix all the ingredients together for the pickling juice with 100ml/3½fl oz/scant 1/2 cup water. Put everything into a bowl and place somewhere cold for one or a couple of hours.

Pickled watermelon rind

Take the opportunity to make use of the rind when making agua fresca (see p.136) and make this super-sour and lovely crunchy pickle that goes well with most things. They're also perfect as a snack on their own or together with a beer in front of the TV, or on a jetty somewhere.

Serves 2–4

1/2 watermelon
200ml/7fl oz/scant 1/2 cup distilled vinegar
200g/7oz/1 cup granulated sugar
1 tbsp salt
1 whole star anise
1 thumb-size piece of fresh ginger

Peel off the green skin from the watermelon and eat everything except 2cm/$^3/_4$in of the pink fruit flesh. You'll now have a watermelon rind made up of about half yellow-green and half pink. Cut the melon into 3–4cm/1$^1/_4$–1$^1/_2$in pieces. Place the rest of the ingredients in a pan with 200ml/7fl oz/scant $^1/_2$ cup and bring to the boil. Add the watermelon and simmer for about 1 minute. Leave to cool, put into a nice jar and place it in the fridge. It's ready to eat after 1 hour and lasts for a week.

Pickled chilli

If you want to put an end to those creepy green-grey, mushy chillies from a jar, it's easy to make your own.

1 jar

350g/12oz fresh red or green chillies, e.g. jalapeño or medium-hot chillies
200ml/7fl oz/generous $^3/_4$ cup cider vinegar
2 tbsp pink peppercorns
2 dried bay leaves
2 garlic cloves
2 tbsp salt
2 tbsp granulated sugar

Slice the chillies into rings with seeds and everything and put into a nice jar. Bring the rest of the ingredients to the boil in a pan with 200ml/7fl oz/generous $^3/_4$ cup water, and simmer for 5 minutes. Pour the hot liquid over the chillies and leave for a couple of hours before putting the jar into the fridge. Will last for a couple of months.

Escabeche

Often served with food in Mexico is a thing called escabeche – which is pieces of pickled super-spicy vegetables.

1 large jar

350g/12oz vegetables, e.g. carrot, radishes and cauliflower (mixed together or separate)
1 red onion
250ml/9fl oz/generous 1 cup cider vinegar
2 tbsp pink peppercorns
2 dried bay leaves
3 garlic cloves
2 tbsp salt
2 tbsp granulated sugar

Peel and cut the vegetables into small bite-sized pieces. Slice the onion. Bring the rest of the ingredients to the boil in a pan with 250ml/9fl oz/generous 1 cup water, add the vegetables, take off the heat and leave on the warm hob for 30 minutes. Leave to cool and put into a nice jar and place in the fridge for one day before you eat it. Will last for a week.

Pickled eggs

Pickled eggs are a classic snack in shabby bars in the American South. For us who don't really have the guts to try them, but would very much like to, here comes a recipe.

Makes 8 snacks

8 eggs
150ml/5fl oz/$^2/_3$ cup white wine vinegar
150ml/5fl oz/$^2/_3$ cup granulated sugar
150ml/5fl oz/$^2/_3$ cup beetroot brine
1 tbsp salt

Hard-boil the eggs and leave to cool. Meanwhile, bring the rest of the ingredients to the boil in a pan with 150ml/5fl oz/$^2/_3$ cup water and leave to cool as well. Peel the eggs, put into a nice jar and pour over the pickling juice. Leave overnight and the eggs will turn into a lovely shocking pink. Will last for a couple of days in the fridge.

Homemade barbecue
INSTRUCTIONS OVERLEAF

HOW TO MAKE A BARBECUE SMOKER

To quick-grill a piece of pork that's been soaking in a ready-made marinade for 30 minutes is always nice – at least once a year. Although for the serious grill-master, there's a whole world of indirect grilling to discover.

When cooking food on the barbecue grill there are two routes to go down: you either go down the more familiar route and grill your sausage, your meat, fish or vegetables using direct heat, where you place whatever you want cooked directly over the coal until it's done.

It's quick, easy and tasty – but not always. Because sometimes you might want a more intense barbecue kick, and that's when it's time to start experimenting with indirect heat – or what the Americans call barbecue.

Indeed, the world's best barbecuing is found in Texas, where in the nineteenth century a unique barbecue culture emerged that is still alive and kicking today. And, as with so many things in America, it's a result of how different groups of people have met and become inspired by each other. Beautiful. German immigrants used to smoke sausages and meat in their home country and brought their food habits to the new country. Gradually the cowboys' 'fire pits' (holes in the ground that food was cooked in on the prairie) as well as the Mexicans' traditional 'barbacoa' were incorporated in the same style.

The result was a cooking method somewhere in between smoking and charcoal grilling and with flavours that at one and the same time reminds you of German 'umpa umpa', country twang and the Mexicans' giant guitars. Delicious.

This sort of barbecue basically means that you cook the meat using indirect heat, with plenty of wood chips for creating lots of yummy smoke in a grill often made out of an oil drum. Firewood is also okay to use of course. The meat is placed in one half of the grill, the charcoal and the wood chips in the other, with a lid down on top so that the heat and the smoke don't escape. The result is an extremely smoky and tender piece

Barbecue in a kettle grill?

Smoke-cooking meat in a kettle grill, does it work? Yes, actually. It's even what that little separator you've probably put away in the garage somewhere is used for. Just place it in the middle of the grill, put the coal on one side and a can of water on the other, and then follow the same instructions as for the barbecue smoker.

of meat that tastes as if a piece of heaven just fell down on your plate.

This method might take a little longer than cooking on a direct heat, but it's actually neither especially difficult nor a lot of effort to cook this way. You just have to sort out the right temperature in the barbecue grill, put on the meat and sit down with a beer or listen to the weather forecast or something. The benefits to gain from this cooking method are also many: in addition to the smoky flavour, the low heat and long cooking time – low and slow are the catchwords – break down the meat fibres so that the more flavourful, but tougher details become tender and amazingly tasty. On the contrary to what one might think, smoke-grilled slow-cooked meat will also be juicier than the quickly prepared piece of meat, when far too much water evaporates.

This means that you need to keep checking the temperature when cooking using indirect heat: a normal oven thermometer that you buy for a tenner in your local homeware store is the indirect barbecue-master's best friend. Control the heat with the amount of charcoal you add, and if it gets too hot, you just have to lift the lid a little (think of an oven). And if you don't want to go all fancy with a super-expensive, commercial smoker barbecue (that will only last for three seasons anyway), it's easy and cheap to make your own.

What you need

Most barbecue-masters in Texas agree: the best smoker grills are the ones you make yourself. Budget about £50 for the material.

Tools

angle grinder
drill
pencil
angle ruler
ruler
spirit level
a good mood

Materials

1 unused oil drum (I do not hold myself liable for any poisoning occurring if you go with a used one)
1 handle
2 hinges
at least 4cm/1½in long male and female screws in suitable widths
4 brackets
1 supporting frame of some sort
1 grill rack

What to do

1 Measure the quarter, or wedge, of the drum that is to be cut out and used as a lid. Look at the picture on the previous spread. Make sure that the drum's screw holes (all drums have these) are positioned down in the grill so that the fire will get some oxygen.
2 Use an angle grinder to cut out your measured wedge.
3 Work out where to put the holes for the hinges and the handle for the lid. Drill and screw together. Do the same thing with the brackets that will support the grill rack.
4 Cut the supporting frame so that the drum can lie down securely. Exactly how to do this depends on what kind of supporting frame you've found. Search in a scrapyard.
5 The grill rack you can either buy second-hand from a scrapyard or new in a shop that sells barbecue accessories. Choose a rack made out of cast iron for best results and remember it should not cover the whole of the grill – if it does, it will be difficult to add more charcoal during cooking.
6 This simple smoker can also be used as a normal barbecue. Just place the coal directly under the meat and grill as usual.

PART 2

BREAKFAST

The most important meal of the day doesn't have to be the most boring. A couple of pancakes with maple syrup and ice cream, or a breakfast taco with a salsa so hot that it grabs you by the collar and cuffs you into shape is, in my opinion, the perfect way to start the day.

CHILAQUILES

Chilaquiles means 'a broken-up old sombrero' (true) and is the Mexicans' hangover breakfast *numero uno*. And it's easy to understand why: it's crispy, eggy and hot.

SERVES 1

2 corn tortillas (see p.12)
2 eggs
salt
a dash of milk
oil, for frying
2–4 tbsp salsa verde (see p.25)
feta cheese
fresh coriander (cilantro)
½ red onion
1 fresh green chilli, e.g. jalapeño
radishes

Either put the corn tortillas in the oven until crispy or deep-fry to nachos. With a fork, whisk together the eggs, salt and milk.

Add the tortilla crisps and mix. Fry the mixture slowly in an oiled frying pan, stirring constantly so that the eggs cover the crisps and everything turns nice and creamy.

Drizzle over the salsa, crumble over the feta, add coriander, onion, chilli and thinly sliced radishes and get started.

Chilaquiles roja

If mixing tortilla crisps in eggs feels a bit weird, you can always do it the other way around – mix them with salsa first, then fry the egg and place on top. There are many variations of this much-loved dish.

Serves 1
2 corn tortillas (see p.12)
2–3 tbsp salsa roja (see p.25)
1 egg
feta cheese

Preheat the oven to 200°C/400°F/Gas mark 6. Cover the tortilla crisps in salsa and bake in the oven for 10 minutes. Fry the egg and place on top. Crumble over the feta.

HUEVOS RANCHEROS

'The ranch owner's eggs' is the name of this incredibly easy, but also incredibly tasty, breakfast. Don't be afraid of the poaching. It doesn't bite. Just remember to use fresh eggs.

SERVES 4

1 tbsp white wine vinegar
4 fresh eggs
4 corn or wheat tortillas (see p.12)
1 batch salsa roja or salsa cocida (see p.25)
feta cheese

Bring a pan of water to the boil, add a dash of vinegar and stir the water with a wooden spoon so that you create a small swirl.

Crack the egg into a small cup and drop it quickly into the water, cover with a lid, take the pan off the heat, and leave the egg for 3 minutes before taking it out using a slotted spoon or skimmer.

Warm up a corn tortilla, add a spoonful of salsa, and top with the poached egg. Grate feta cheese on top like a boss.

Huevos divorciados

Literally means divorced eggs – but instead of infidelity, it's one green and one red salsa that keep them apart in this instance. Clever.

Serves 1
2 eggs
1 corn tortilla
1–2 tbsp salsa verde (see p.25)
1–2 tbsp salsa roja (see p.25)

Fry the eggs and place them on top of the tortilla. Dollop one kind of salsa over each egg.

TEX-MEX PANCAKES

There are endless variations of American pancakes, but if you want to save some time, I can tell you that these three are the absolute most scrumptious ones: banana pancakes, coconut and lime pancakes, and lastly cinnamon and apple pancakes.

SERVES 4

250g/9oz/1¾ cups plain (all-purpose) flour
2 tsp baking powder
½ tsp salt
1 tbsp granulated sugar
250ml/9fl oz/generous 1 cup milk
2 tbsp melted butter + butter for frying
1 egg

COCONUT AND LIME PANCAKE
250g/9oz/2¾ cups toasted desiccated (dry unsweetened) coconut
finely grated zest and juice of 1 lime
1 tsp ground cinnamon

BANANA PANCAKE
2–3 bananas

CINNAMON AND APPLE PANCAKE
2 apples
2 tbsp butter
2 tbsp soft brown sugar
1 tbsp ground cinnamon

Mix the dry ingredients for the batter together. Add the milk and whisk, followed by the melted butter and finally the egg.

If you want to make coconut and lime pancakes, add the coconut, lime and cinnamon straight to the batter.

If you want to make banana pancakes, slice the bananas and press them down on the pancake just after you've put the batter in the pan.

And if you want to make cinnamon apples, slice the apples and fry them over a medium heat together with the butter, sugar and cinnamon for about 10 minutes or until soft. Place the fried apples on top of the finished pancakes like a turbo-fuelled jam.

As for the pancakes, fry them in a knob of butter in a frying pan. When you see bubbles appearing on the top, it's time to flip them over. Make them either normal sized (about 10cm/4in) or as silver dollars (mini-versions).

Serve with maple syrup and vanilla ice cream, shop-bought or homemade (see p.116).

BREAKFAST TACO

Tacos for breakfast? Is that really possible? Yes, it's not only possible, it's even encouraged, especially when they're as good as this one. Skip the beer though. That would be a bad idea. Or, would it?

SERVES 1

1 small piece uncooked chorizo
1 potato
oil, for frying
2 eggs
1 tsp milk
salt
1 dollop of butter
1–2 tbsp salsa roja (see p.25)
2–4 small corn tortillas (see p.12)

Tip!

The taco is easily transformed into a breakfast burrito if you swap the sausage for bacon and the corn tortilla for wheat. Drizzle over the salsa.

Remove the skin from the uncooked chorizo, then crumble into small pieces and fry until nice and crispy. You don't need frying oil. The chorizo is fatty enough.

Peel and cut the potato into tiny little matchstick shapes and deep-fry in hot oil until golden and crispy. Drain on a piece of kitchen paper.

Make scrambled eggs by whisking together the eggs with a dash of milk and some salt, and fry super-slowly in butter over a low heat while stirring constantly until nice and creamy.

Build the breakfast taco by first spreading the tortilla with salsa, then add a dollop of scrambled eggs, sausage and top with a pile of potatoes. Delicious.

PART 3

ANTOJITOS

The word 'antojitos' means that feeling you have when you're a bit peckish and want a small bite of something – and peckish is just what you will feel when getting introduced to these Tex-Mex snacks. Everything from enchiladas via nachos to tostados.

TRUCK STOP ENCHILADA

'Svenne tacos' is a watered-down Swedish variation of American fast-food chain tacos, which in turn are a watered-down version of Mexican cuisine. But in neither genuine Tex-Mex nor Mex is beef mince used – it's a lazy shortcut to achieve that stringy, melt-in-the-mouth consistency of the slow-cooked meat used in a genuine chilli.

SERVES 6

12 large wheat tortillas (see p.12)
1 batch salsa roja (see p.25)
1 batch beef chilli (see p.70)
200g/7oz/1¾ cups Cheddar or Manchego cheese, grated
200g/7oz/1¾ cups mozzarella, grated

Preheat the oven to 200°C/400°F/Gas mark 6. Dip the tortilla bread in the salsa – enchiladas literally means 'dipped in chilli' – add a dollop of beef chilli and most of the cheese.

Roll together and place in an ovenproof dish. Drizzle over the remaining salsa, sprinkle over the rest of the cheese, and bake in the oven for 10 minutes, or until it's bubbling.

Serve with *chopped coriander (cilantro), white onion and crème fraîche.*

BAJA CEVICHE

There are few things that taste of summer as much as dipping tortilla crisps into a bowl of lime-marinated, raw fish. To make the snazzy ice bowls on p. 50: put ice cubes into a bowl, press a smaller bowl among the ice, fill it up with water and then put the whole lot in the freezer.

SERVES 6

CLASSIC CEVICHE

500g/1lb/2oz firm white fish of sushi standard, e.g. halibut
300ml/10fl oz/1¼ cups freshly squeezed lime juice
1 white onion
2 fresh chillies, e.g. medium-hot chillies or jalapeños
100g/3½oz/½ cup green olives
1 large tomato
1 large bunch of fresh coriander (cilantro)
2 tbsp olive oil
salt

GREEN CUCUMBER CEVICHE

500g/1lb 2oz firm white fish of sushi standard, e.g. halibut
1 batch green herby salsa (see p.26)
100ml/3½fl oz/scant ½ cup freshly squeezed lime juice

CLASSIC CEVICHE

Cut the fish into cubes and leave to 'cook' in the lime juice for 30–60 minutes in the fridge. If you're a bit of a wuss, you can leave them for up to 3 hours, but then the fish will be cooked all the way through (that's what lime does to it). Use a stainless-steel bowl or a glass bowl. Drain off the lime, finely chop the vegetables and coriander, and add to the fish together with the olive oil and mix. Add salt to taste. Eat within 1 hour.

GREEN CUCUMBER CEVICHE

Cut the fish into dipping-friendly sized cubes and mix together with the salsa and the lime juice. Leave to marinate for at least 30 minutes, maximum 1 hour.

Serve with *deep-fried corn tortilla crisps (see p.13) to scoop it up with.*

Naco de Nachos

Nachos with melted cheese we all know, right? This variation is much tastier and can, depending on how much cheese you add, be both a calorie bomb and actually quite healthy.

SERVES 4

250g/9oz flank or sirloin steak
salt and freshly ground black pepper
oil, for frying
4 small corn tortillas (see p.12)
grated cheese, either feta or Cheddar

SOY MARINADE
200ml/7fl oz/generous 3/4 cup diluted pineapple juice
freshly squeezed juice of 1 lime
100ml/3½fl oz/scant ½ cup Japanese soy sauce
1 tsp chopped garlic
1 tsp ground cumin
salt and freshly ground black pepper

REFRIED BEANS
1 dried chipotle chilli
3 garlic cloves
½ brown onion
½ pack (70g/2¾oz) bacon rashers (slices)
corn oil, for frying
2 tsp ground cumin
1 tsp dried oregano
1 can (410g/14oz) black beans, drained
salt and freshly ground black pepper

Serve with chunky guacamole (see p.17), chopped coriander (cilantro) and white onion or your choice of pickles.

Combine the ingredients for the marinade and leave the meat to marinate for at least 1 hour. Grill quickly on a barbecue or using a griddle. Season with salt and pepper.

To make the refried beans, remove the stalk and deseed the dried chilli, cover with 100–200ml/3½–7fl oz/scant ½–generous ¾ cup water and boil for about 15 minutes. Meanwhile, chop and fry the garlic and onion together with the bacon in a little oil. Season with the cumin and oregano and add the can of drained black beans. Mix the chipotle and the water together in a blender, add to the bean mixture and leave to cook over a low heat for about 15 minutes. Add a bit more water if needed. Add salt and pepper to taste. Then mash about a third of the beans with a fork and stir.

Now you have two options: preheat the oven to maximum. Either place the tortillas on a baking tray and spread the beans on top. Cut the grilled meat into fine strips and place on top. Feta if you want to take it easy, Cheddar if you want to crank it up. Place in the oven for 6 minutes, or until the cheese has melted and the tortilla looks crunchy. Take out and cut into 4 pieces.

Or, divide the tortilla into 4 pieces, deep-fry them and place the bean mixture, the meat and the cheese on top and chuck it in the oven. Don't forget the beer, you silly goose.

Tortilla soup
RECIPE OVERLEAF

TORTILLA SOUP

The problem with soup, right, is that it's very rarely crispy. This ingenious soup, however, is at the same time comfortingly hot and satisfyingly crunchy – a personal favourite.

SERVES 4–6

1 whole (about 1.3kg/3lb) chicken
5 tomatoes
5 brown onions
5–6 fresh red or green chillies, e.g. medium-hot chillies or jalapeños
3 garlic cloves
1 large bunch of fresh coriander (cilantro)
2 carrots
3 celery sticks
3 potatoes
8 small corn tortillas (see p.12)
oil, for deep-frying
4 avocados
1 lime
1 white onion
salt

Tips!

The corn tortilla cannot be replaced with wheat tortilla, but in a worst case scenario they can be replaced with shop-bought tortilla crisps.

Half the chicken and boil in 2 litres/$3^{1}/_{2}$ pints/$8^{1}/_{2}$ cups water for about 1 hour.

Preheat the oven to 225°C/437°F/Gas mark 7. Cut the tomatoes, 1 onion, 2 chillies and the garlic into large chunks. Place on a baking tray and bake in the oven for about 10 minutes. Once they've got a bit of colour, put everything in a blender together with half of the coriander. Take the chicken out of the water and remove any debris and fat floating around on the surface.

Dice the carrots, the remaining onions, the celery and potatoes. Add the root vegetables and the tomato sauce to the chicken stock and bring to the boil. Reduce the heat and simmer for about 25 minutes. Meanwhile, cut the corn tortillas into fine strips and deep-fry until golden and crispy. Dice the avocado and put into a bowl, slice the remaining chillies and put into another one. Cut the lime into wedges and put into a bowl and chop the white onion and the remaining coriander and, that's right, put into a bowl.

Pick the meat off the chicken, give the skin to the dog, then tear the meat into smaller bits and put into a bowl. Serve by letting your guests fill their soup bowl with meat and the other trimmings. Season the soup with salt and ladle over the chicken. Garnish with a handful of the deep-fried tortilla crisps.

SHRIMP TAQUITOS

Shrimp taquitos are small crispy corn tortilla wraps that are the perfect finger food and extremely dip friendly. Just make sure you use very thin corn tortillas, preferably bought from a Latin American shop or specialist deli. Or else they can break.

SERVES 6

1/2 white onion
2 garlic cloves
1–2 fresh red or green chillies, e.g. medium-hot chillies
1 tbsp olive oil
2 tomatoes
200–300g/7–11oz/1 2/3–2 1/2 cups fresh peeled prawns (shrimp)
1 small bunch of fresh coriander (cilantro)
oil, for deep-frying
12 thin small corn tortillas (see p.12)
200g/7oz/1 3/4 cups mozzarella, grated
salt

Finely chop and fry the onion, garlic and chillies in the oil until soft. Blanch the tomatoes and remove the skin as well as the seeds. Chop and fry together with the onion mix until you get a consistency similar to ketchup.

Chop the prawns and add to the mixture. Add finely chopped coriander.

Heat the oil for deep-frying to about 185°C/365°F. Dip the corn tortilla into the oil for about 1 second to soften. Spread about 3 tablespoons of the prawn mixture on each tortilla, sprinkle over the mozzarella, roll together into a cigar-like wrap and skewer in pairs on a soaked bamboo skewer so that you've got something to hold on to.

Deep-fry until crispy, for about 2 minutes, and season with salt. Get dipping.

Serve with salsa of your choice (see p.24) and perhaps a guacamole (see p.17).

El Mistico

ENCHILADAS SUIZAS

Despite the name, this is not Swiss enchiladas, they're just called so because of the crème fraîche-based sauce. If you can't find fresh tomatillos, you can use canned ones or even a mix of unripe tomatoes and physalis or Cape gooseberries. The important thing is to get the acidity right.

SERVES 4

300ml/10fl oz/1¼ cups chicken stock (broth)
200ml/7fl oz/generous ¾ cup crème fraîche
1 batch salsa verde (see p.25)
salt and freshly ground black pepper
2 potatoes
2 carrots
1 swede (rutabaga)
3 tbsp olive oil, plus extra for drizzling
400g/14oz uncooked chorizo
6 large or 12 small wheat tortillas (see p.12)
100g/3½oz/scant 1 cup Cheddar or Manchego, grated
100g/3½oz/scant 1 cup mozzarella, grated

Preheat the oven to 200°C/400°F/Gas mark 6. Add the chicken stock and crème fraîche to a batch of salsa verde, then season with salt and pepper.

Dice the root vegetables into 1cm/½in cubes, drizzle with olive oil, sprinkle over salt and roast in the oven until crispy, about 20 minutes.

Remove the skin from the uncooked chorizo and crumble the meat into a hot pan with the 3 tablespoons olive oil and fry until cooked.

Assemble the enchilada by dipping the tortilla in the salsa, put the sausage and root vegetables on top, roll into a wrap and place side by side in an ovenproof dish. Alternatively, if you use small tortillas, stack into a pile instead, like a round lasagne (see picture). This is called a stacked enchilada and is a method often used in New Mexico. Drizzle over the rest of the salsa, add the grated cheeses and bake for about 10 minutes or until the cheese is golden.

Serve with chopped white onion, crème fraîche and fresh coriander (cilantro).

Tres tostadas

RECIPE OVERLEAF

Tres Tostadas

A tostada is simply a deep-fried corn tortilla with lots of lovely goodies on top – so not too far from a crispy taco (minus the silly curve). Eat it like a Mexican crisp bread.

Creamy lobster tostada

Lobster, mayonnaise, chilli – you get the idea.

Makes 4 tostadas

1 fresh poblano chilli (or 1 pointed pepper and 1 standard fresh chilli)
4 garlic cloves
3 tbsp mayonnaise
salt
1 whole boiled lobster
4 corn tortillas (see p.12)
oil, for deep-frying
½ batch pico de gallo (see p.26)

Roast the poblano chilli/pointed pepper together with the garlic (keep the skin on). They're ready when the skin is black. Peel and blend together with the mayonnaise. Season with salt to taste and stir in the lobster meat. Deep-fry a whole corn tortilla and drain on a piece of kitchen paper. Top with a spoonful of salsa and some lobster mixture and eat.

Devil shrimp tostada

These hot and buttery prawns also make a tasty taco-filler (like everything else).

Makes 4 tostadas

salt and freshly ground black pepper
1–2 tsp chilli powder
5 garlic cloves
2–3 tbsp butter
200–300g/7–11oz/3–2½ cups peeled fresh prawns (shrimp)
1 lime
4 corn tortillas (see p.12)
oil, for deep-frying
½ batch salsa para mariscos (see p.26)

Mash salt, pepper, chilli powder and garlic together using a pestle and mortar. Melt the butter in a frying pan and fry off the garlic mixture. Add the peeled prawns and warm through, for 1 minute max. Not too long, or they will go dry. Squeeze lime on top. Deep-fry a whole corn tortilla and drain on a piece of kitchen paper. Top with a spoonful of salsa and some prawns and eat.

Green scallop tostada

Ceviche-style tostada

Makes 4 tostadas

3–4 limes
3 fresh chillies, e.g. jalapeños
salt 300g/11oz fresh scallops
½ cucumber
1 bunch of radishes
4 corn tortillas (see p.12)
oil, for deep-frying

Squeeze the lime and mix together with the chillies until a green juice appears. Strain to get rid of the bits and season with salt. Thinly slice the scallops and leave to marinate in the lime juice for up to 1 hour. Peel the cucumber, remove the seeds and slice thinly. Slice the radishes too. Deep-fry a whole corn tortilla and drain on a piece of kitchen paper. Top with the stuff.

Tips!

Make a batch pickled watermelon rind (see p.30) to go with your tostadas. Don't forget the beer.

Right: Pickled watermelon rind (p.30)

PART 4

TACOS

A taco served with an ice-cold beer must be the best street food in the world. So scrumptious, so portable and so rich in variation; almost anything can be stuffed in between a couple of tortilla breads, and almost anything is. Turn the page to find out how to make the world's best taco at home.

BEEF CHILLI TACO

Francis X Tolbert was an American chilli lover who dedicated his life to finding the perfect chilli recipe. And this is what he discovered: no tomato, no beans and just a whole lot of chilli. And this chilli is hot, of course, but it's a kind of muffled rumbling heat, almost caressing.

SERVES 4

1 dried chipotle chilli
1–2 dried chillies, e.g. ancho
about 1kg/2¼lb braising steak
1 whole garlic
corn oil, for frying
2–3 tbsp plain (all-purpose) flour
1 tbsp chilli powder
2 tsp dried oregano
2 tsp ground cumin
2 tsp dried coriander
1 tbsp granulated sugar
salt and freshly ground black pepper
1–2 fresh chillies
330ml/11fl oz/1½ cups lager
1 beef stock (bouillon) cube

Remove the stalks and seeds from the dried chillies. Cover with 100–200ml/3½–7fl oz/ scant ½–generous ¾ cup water and boil for about 15 minutes. Dice the braising steak and finely chop the garlic, then fry the meat and garlic in a little oil. Fry a small bit at a time to get a nice searing of the meat.

Dust the fried meat with flour, chilli powder, the other dried herbs and spices, the sugar and salt and pepper. Finely chop and add the fresh chillies. Whiz the boiled chillies and water together in a blender and pour over the stew. Add the lager and stock cube so that it just covers the meat.

Cover with a lid and leave to simmer for at least 2 hours, or until the meat is tender and thready.

Serve with small wheat or corn tortillas (see p.12), wedges of lime, crème fraîche, chopped coriander (cilantro), white onion and grated Cheddar cheese.

GREEN SCALLOP TACO

There's something satisfying about matching the colour of different foods, right? This super-easy salsa (also great on your breakfast eggs) has a beautiful green hulk colour so do choose a fresh green chilli so you don't ruin that effect.

SERVES 4

16 fresh scallops
salt and freshly ground black pepper
groundnut (peanut) oil, for frying
butter, for frying
1 batch green herby salsa (see p.26)
lime juice, to taste

Tip!

If you don't want to fry the scallops, do a ceviche instead – just marinate in lime juice for 10 minutes.

Pat the scallops with some kitchen paper until completely dry (if they're wet, they won't turn a nice colour). Season with salt and pepper and place in a really hot pan with some groundnut oil in. Now for the tricky bit: you must absolutely not move them about, and at the same time you'd of course like a nice caramelised crust that isn't burnt. So how do you do it? Well, wait a couple of minutes and when your intuition says they're starting to get done, lift one of them carefully and take a peak underneath. If it looks the same as in a restaurant, you flip them over, add a dollop of butter and leave to sear on the other side as well – at the same time as you spoon over the melted butter from the pan. Tasty!

Remember that a thoroughly cooked scallop is not an alternative so if you don't like half-cooked seafood do another recipe instead.

When they're done: place 2 scallops on each tortilla, spoon over the salsa, squeeze over lime juice to taste and enjoy.

Serve with *small wheat or corn tortillas (see p.12) and lime wedges.*

TACO AL PASTOR

Taco al pastor is a little bit like the Mexican equivalent of kebab. A marinated piece of meat that spins around with a pineapple on top, so the juices are dripping down, adding a sweetness to the meat and also working as a natural tenderiser. Yum! But it also works well to make al pastor at home.

SERVES 4

1 tsp cumin seeds
½ tsp dried oregano
2 large garlic cloves
1 white onion
2 dried chillies, e.g. ancho
5–10 other dried chillies depending on strength and taste
2 tbsp cider vinegar
2 tsp salt
2 tbsp freshly squeezed lime juice
1 pineapple, peeled with stem removed
1kg/2¼lb pork collar (neck) without the bone

Preheat the oven to maximum. Toast the cumin seeds in a dry pan and crush together with the oregano in a pestle and mortar (or use ground cumin if you're lazy). Leave to the side. Put the garlic and half of the white onion (save the other half) on a baking tray without oil and place in the oven until they've got colour.

Halve the dried chillies, remove the stalks and seeds, and boil in 100–200ml/3½–7fl oz/scant ½–generous ¾ cup water for about 15 minutes. Blend everything together and add the crushed spices, vinegar, salt, lime juice, half of the pineapple (save the other half until later), the roasted onion and garlic and blend. Leave to cool.

Slice the pork, drizzle with half of the marinade (save the other half in the fridge) and leave to marinate for 4 hours or overnight. When it's time to eat, slice the saved half of the pineapple and grill on a hot griddle. Take the meat out of the marinade and let it drain a little, then grill quickly over a high heat. Slice the meat thinly and serve with the saved marinade slightly heated up. But don't use the one the meat's marinated in, silly. Or you might end up with a bellyache.

Serve with small wheat or corn tortillas (see p.12), salsa verde or salsa roja (see p.25), as well as chopped white onion.

BAJA FISH TACO

Fish and coleslaw might not sound that super-appetising, but I promise you – baja fish taco is the king of tacos.

SERVES 4

100g/3½oz/¾ cup plain (all-purpose) flour
2 tsp chilli powder
2 tsp ground cumin
1 tbsp paprika
salt
1 egg
100g/3½oz/¾ cup panko breadcrumbs (or more if needed)
oil, for deep-frying
600g/1¼lb fish fillets, e.g. tuna steak, sea bass or halibut

COLESLAW
1 tbsp freshly squeezed lime juice
1 tbsp Dijon mustard
2 garlic cloves, crushed
2 egg yolks
200ml/7fl oz/generous ¾ cup corn oil
lime zest, to taste
salt and freshly ground black pepper
¼ red or white cabbage

Mix the lime juice, mustard, garlic and egg yolks together for the coleslaw. Pour the oil into the mix very slowly while whisking with an electric whisk. Be careful so it doesn't split. Add lime zest and salt and pepper to taste.

Finely shred the cabbage and mix with the aïoli – don't use too much, just so the cabbage is covered. Put it in the fridge.

Just before it's time to eat, mix the flour and the spices together on a plate, whisk the egg and put on another plate and put the panko on a third. Heat a couple of centimetres of oil in a frying pan or a saucepan with high edges. Dip the fish fillets in the spiced flour first, then in the egg and lastly in the panko. Drop into the hot oil. Deep-fry for a couple of minutes on each side, until the panko breadcrumbs have turned a nice colour then drain on a piece of kitchen paper.

Serve with small wheat or corn tortillas (see p.12), mango salsa (see p.26) and crumbled feta cheese.

CARNITA TACO

'Carnita' literally means 'little meats' and it's just what this is – pork boiled in Coca-Cola and spices until transformed into a thready, chewy and sweet-spicy goo that you will love for the rest of your life.

SERVES 4

1kg/2¼lb pork collar (neck) without the bone
2 tbsp fuego spice mix (see p.21)
1 lime
1 orange
1 tbsp Chinese soy sauce
1 tbsp ground cumin
5 garlic cloves
500ml/18fl oz/generous 2 cups Coca-Cola (not diet)

Cut the pork into small cubes and massage the fuego spice mix into the meat. Squeeze over lime and orange, then add soy and cumin. Finely chop and add the garlic and leave to marinate for at least 1 hour, but preferably overnight.

Take the meat out of the marinade, save the marinade and fry the meat. Once the meat's got colour, you can add the marinade. Open the Coca-Cola and pour in until the meat is covered. Top up when needed. Cover with a lid and simmer for at least 2 hours.

Remove the lid towards the end and leave to cook until you've got a lovely, sticky goo.

Serve with small wheat or corn tortillas (see p.12), guacamole of your choice (see p.17) and mango salsa (see p.26).

CRISPY PRAWN TACO

Fried king prawns are scrumptious. But make sure they're wild caught. Anything else is just evil. If you can't find any, you can use normal cooked prawns or firm white fish cut into prawn size. Don't forget the quick pickled carrots to go with it.

SERVES 4

100g/3½oz/¾ cup plain (all-purpose) flour
1 tsp salt
1 egg
1 tbsp milk
200g/7oz/scant 1½ cups panko breadcrumbs
oil, for deep-frying
200–300g/7–11oz/3–2½ cups peeled fresh prawns (shrimp)

CHILLI MAYO
1 tbsp Dijon mustard
1 tbsp freshly squeezed lime juice
2 garlic cloves, crushed
2 egg yolks
200ml/7fl oz/generous ¾ cup corn oil
salt and freshly ground black pepper
1–2 tbsp pickled chilli (see p.31)

Make a mayonnaise by mixing together the mustard, lime juice, garlic and egg yolks. Pour the oil into the mixture very slowly while whisking with an electric whisk. Be careful so it doesn't split. Add salt and pepper to taste. Blend home-pickled chilli until smooth and stir into the mayonnaise. Take a second to feel proud of your homemade mayo before getting started on the pickled carrots.

When food-time is closing in, just mix the flour and salt on a plate, whisk the egg and put on another plate and put the panko breadcrumbs on a third. Heat a couple of centimetres of oil in a frying pan or a saucepan with high edges. Dip the prawns in the spiced flour first, then in the egg and lastly in the panko breadcrumbs. To jazz it up a bit, you can leave the tails unpeeled. Drop into the hot oil and deep-fry for about 1 minute on each side until the panko breadcrumbs have turned a nice colour, then drain on a piece of kitchen paper.

Serve with small wheat or corn tortillas (see p.12), thinly sliced avocados, white onion and some lime wedges.

BEER-BRAISED LAMB SHANK TACO

Everyone likes dipping, right (hey, you!)? And there are few things that are nicer to dip in than the juices left over from beer braising some lamb shank. So pour it into a bowl and serve on the side.

SERVES 4

3 tbsp chilli powder
2 tbsp ground cumin
1 tbsp dried coriander
½ tbsp ground cinnamon
about 1.5kg/3¼lb medium-sized lamb shanks on the bone
corn oil, for frying
660ml/just over 1 pint/3 cups dark beer
4 tbsp cider vinegar
2 tbsp tomato purée (paste)
salt and freshly ground black pepper

Mix the dry ingredients in a bowl and pat onto the lamb shanks.

Sear the shanks in oil for 2–3 minutes on each side in a cast-iron casserole dish. Reduce the heat and add the beer, vinegar and tomato purée. Cover with a lid and leave to simmer for 2–4 hours. Remove the lid towards the end of cooking and reduce the braising juices a little. Add salt and pepper to taste.

Pull the meat off the bone with a fork and serve together with the braising juices that you can pour into a bowl on the side for dipping the tacos.

Serve with small wheat or corn tortillas (see p.12), thinly sliced avocados, white onion and some lime wedges.

PART 5

BARBECUES

What do you get if you mix the Germans' sausage smoking with the Mexicans' *barbacoa* and the cowboys' fire pits? Answer: the world's best barbecue culture. Turn the page for a mouthwatering basic course.

PULLED PORK

Pulled pork is a barbecue classic and all it needs is bread, coleslaw and perhaps some crispy pork crackling as accompaniments. It's a dish worthy of a barbecue-craving king or queen. It will, of course, taste nicer cooked on an outdoor barbecue than in the oven.

SERVES 4

about 1.2kg/2¾lb pork collar (neck) on the bone
barbecue rub (see p.22)

Cook on indirect heat

For exact method see p.34.

Serve with homemade burger buns (see p.13-4), apple coleslaw (see p.105) and barbecue sauce (see p.105). Alternatively, with homemade burger buns, taco shop guacamole (see p.18), and pickled red onion (see p.30).

OUTDOOR BARBECUE:
Massage the barbecue rub into the meat before placing it on the part of the grill that hasn't got any charcoal underneath. It shouldn't get too hot, 110–120°C/230–248°F. (Don't cheat.) The sugar in the rub will caramelise into a hard coating that makes the outside crispy and the inside juicy. Place a plate filled with water underneath the meat so that it doesn't get too dry, throw a handful of wood-smoking chips on the burning charcoal and cover with the lid. Throw a couple of handfuls of wood chips over the coal every 30 minutes for about 2½ hours. Wrap the meat in aluminium foil and grill on an indirect heat until the meat starts to break off when you're poking it but is still juicy. Allow 2–3 hours per kilogram of meat.

OVEN:
Preheat the oven to 110°C/230°F/Gas mark ¼ (use an oven thermometer). Massage the barbecue rub into the meat before placing it in an ovenproof dish and roasting in the oven. Roast until the inside temperature reaches 95°C/203°F, which could take up to 6 hours, then turn the oven off and leave the roast in the oven to cool for about 2 hours.

WHEN THE MEAT IS DONE:
Leave to rest and finely pull it apart using two forks. It should break easily and be nice and thready. If you want, you can mix in a bit more of the spice mix.

CARNE ASADA

Grilled meat and some guaca, it doesn't have to be more complicated than that to throw a party. Both onglet and flank steak are chewy but incredibly rich in flavour (and cheap). The kiwi in the marinade contains an enzyme that tenderises the meat.

SERVES 4

1 whole (about 1kg/2¼lb) onglet (hanger) or flank steak

MARINADE
juice of 1 lime
50ml/2fl oz/scant ¼ cup olive oil
1 small bunch of fresh coriander (cilantro)
1 fresh red or green chilli, e.g. medium-hot chilli
½ kiwi fruit
3 garlic cloves
1 tsp granulated sugar
½ tsp dried oregano
¼ tsp ground cumin
2 tsp salt
freshly ground black pepper

Mix all the ingredients for the marinade together and leave the meat to marinate overnight.

OUTDOOR BARBECUE:
Just before lighting the barbecue, take the meat out of the fridge and leave at room temperature. When the flames have died down and the charcoals are white and hot, place the meat directly above. Throw a couple of handfuls of soaked mesquite wood chips on the coals and close the lid so your meat gets that really smoky flavour as well as the lovely red colour. Grill for a couple of minutes on each side and remove the meat while it feels juicy, leave to rest for 5 minutes, and slice thinly, across the fibres of the meat.

OVEN:
Preheat the oven to 200°C/400°F/Gas mark 6. It also works to cook on a griddle on the hob – but remember the pan has to be so hot that it's smoking. Finish off by placing the meat in the oven for a couple of minutes.

Serve with small wheat or corn tortillas (see p.12), chunky guacamole (see p.17), crumbled feta cheese and pickled red onion (see p.30).

Chilli Cheeseburger

A really good burger should be crispy on the outside and so juicy inside that you have to lean over the plate when taking the first bite. The secret is not adding a secret ingredient, but the other way around, it's what you don't add. For a real burger has only three ingredients: beef, salt and freshly ground black pepper.

SERVES 4

800g/1¾lb freshly minced (ground) beef with 20–30% fat, e.g. braising steak, brisket or flank steak
salt and freshly ground black pepper
2 green pointed peppers
2–3 fresh green chillies
4 slices of pre-sliced Cheddar cheese
4 homemade burger buns (see p.13-14)

Serve with ketchup, mustard and mayonnaise mixed together to a simple hamburger sauce as well as thinly sliced white onion.

Go to the butcher and buy a cheap but fatty bit of meat like braising steak, brisket or flank steak and ask them to mince (grind) it. When you're back home, mix this glorious mince with salt and pepper to form burgers. This is good meat so you can go ahead and taste it to check it's seasoned well. Get the barbecue going. Char the pointed peppers and the chillies until the skins turn black, place in a plastic bag and after a couple of minutes, peel the skins off and chop roughly.

OUTDOOR BARBECUE:
Grill the burgers directly over the white charcoal without piercing them with a fork so the juices escape. Do not press them down with the turner either, burgers should be juicy and light, not rock-hard ice hockey pucks. When they bounce like the tip of your nose, they're medium cooked. Place the chopped chillies and a slice of cheese on top and leave to melt. Then just put it between two pieces of bread and enjoy.

FRYING PAN:
If you want to cook your burgers in a frying pan, that's fine too. Just use a cast-iron pan that's so hot it's smoking. Add some oil and flip the burgers every 20 seconds, they'll get juicier that way, until they feel medium cooked.

LEGS OF FIRE

This has to be the best barbecue chicken in the world, as it contains elements from every part of the Tex-Mex cuisine's food circle: it's crispy, hot, sweet, fun and sticky. You can also use wings and thighs for this recipe. Probably breast too, but seriously, who would want that?

SERVES 4

1–1.5kg/2¼–3¼lb chicken legs
100ml/3½fl oz/scant ½ cup olive oil
1 tbsp paprika
1 tsp chilli powder
1 tsp cayenne pepper
1 tsp garlic powder
1 tsp ground white pepper
1 tsp dried oregano
1 tsp salt
barbecue sauce (see p.105)

OUTDOOR BARBECUE:
Rub the chicken with the oil and the other dry spices and fry over a direct heat until the juices are running clear.

Drizzle the barbecue sauce over the chicken and finish off on the barbecue until the skin is so crispy that the neighbours complain.

OVEN:
Preheat the oven to 175°C/347°F/Gas mark 5. Rub the chicken with the oil and the other dry spices and roast in the oven for 30 minutes. Drizzle over the barbecue sauce and turn up the oven to max until everything is nice and crispy.

Serve with guacamole con piña y pepino (see p.18) and tortilla crisps (see p.13).

BEER CAN CHICKEN

To cook a chicken placed on a beer can might sound like gastronomy for banjo players – but the truth is that it's a perfect way to get a flavourful and juicy bird. This is because the beer evaporates inside the chicken and contributes with both moisture and a nice flavour. In combination with the barbecue's slow and smoky cooking qualities, the end result is super magnifico.

SERVES 4

1 whole (about 1.3kg/3lb) chicken
corn oil
rendez-vous dry rub (see p.21)
500ml/18fl oz/generous 2 cups beer

Cook on indirect heat

For exact method see p.34.

Pat the chicken with the oil and the spice mix. Leave to marinate for 1 hour in the fridge. Meanwhile, prepare the barbecue for indirect cooking – fill one half with charcoal, in the other half place a pan of water. Drink half of the beer and place the bird on top with the can in its cavity. Then place the can on the half of the barbecue that hasn't got any charcoal in it. Throw a couple of handfuls of mesquite chips on the coals and close the lid. After 30 minutes, throw in another handful. That should do it for smoke now. Leave the chicken to cook slowly and steadily for 3–4 hours at around 110–112°C/230–234°F. The inside temperature of the chicken should be 75–80°C/167–176°F.

Serve with poblano potato salad (see p.105).

MEMPHIS DRY RIBS

To barbecue really delicious ribs is significantly easier than one might think. You do need some patience though; a six-pack of beer, some music and a garden recliner while you're waiting. Dry ribs are spare ribs cooked without barbecue sauce on a direct heat but with a spice mix that is massaged into the meat, that as a result becomes crispier and chewier than normal sticky ribs.

SERVES 4

2kg/4½lb baby back ribs
200ml/7fl oz/generous ¾ cup water
200ml/7fl oz/generous ¾ cup white wine vinegar
rendez-vous dry rub, p.21

OUTDOOR BARBECUE:
Mix together 200ml/7fl oz/generous ¾ cup water, the vinegar and a couple of tablespoons of the rub. When the charcoals are white, it's time to start barbecuing. Dry ribs are grilled over a direct heat – with the grill rack straight over the charcoals – and should cook for 1 hour. If it gets too hot, move them over to the indirect side. To avoid burning the ribs, use the vinegar mixture for tenderising the meat, keeping it juicy and cooling it down. Do it regularly throughout the whole grilling process and make sure it doesn't burn. After 1 hour, sprinkle over more spice mix and serve.

OVEN:
Preheat the oven to 200°C/400°F/Gas mark 6. Cook for 45–60 minutes. Make sure to turn the ribs over regularly and cool down with the vinegar mixture.

Serve with elotes (see p.105), and/or guacamole of your choice (see p.17), and tortilla crisps (see p.13).

TEXAS WET RIBS

Real barbecue ribs are fantastically tasty, tender and juicy, but contrary to popular belief, they don't melt in your mouth. So don't try to cheat by pre-boiling the meat – it's only half-shabby barbecue restaurants that do that.

SERVES 4

1 tbsp paprika
1 tsp chilli powder
1 tsp cayenne pepper
1 tsp garlic powder
1 tsp ground white pepper
1 tsp dried oregano
1 tsp salt
2kg/4½lb baby back ribs
3 tbsp corn oil
barbecue sauce (see p.105)

Cook on indirect heat

For exact method see p.34.

Serve with elotes (see p.105), and/or guacamole of your choice (see p.17), and tortilla crisps (see p.13).

OUTDOOR BARBECUE:
Mix together the dry spices and rub into the meat together with the oil. You could leave it to marinate for 1 hour (or don't bother). Prepare the barbecue by placing charcoal in one half. Don't use too much, the temperature should be about 110–120°C/230–248°F. Put the meat in the other half with a bowl of water underneath. Throw a couple of handfuls of mesquite wood chips over the coals and close the lid. After 30 minutes, throw another couple of handfuls in. Now, that's enough, 1 hour is all you need so that the meat doesn't get over-smoked. Leave the ribs to cook on the barbecue until the meat is tender and juicy – for large ribs, allow 4–5 hours – for small ones, 3 hours are enough. Add more charcoal when needed and turn the ribs over from time to time. When the meat has turned a nice colour and seems to begin falling off the bone – you need a bit of bite though – it's time to start brushing the ribs with the barbecue sauce and placing the rack directly over the charcoals. Cook on direct heat for a couple of minutes or until the barbecue sauce has caramelised.

OVEN:
Preheat the oven to 110°C/225°F/Gas mark ¼. First, cook in the oven for the same time as above, then cover with barbecue sauce and turn the oven to max until it's caramelised.

BARBECUE SIDES

A human can't live on barbecued food only (unfortunately). So here are a few classic barbecue sides.

Poblano potato salad

Creamy potato salad with a spicy twist

1kg/2¼lb new potatoes
2–3 tbsp corn oil
1 whole garlic
2 large fresh poblano chillies or 1 large pointed pepper and 1 fresh chilli
2 tbsp mayonnaise
4 salad onions
salt
3 tbsp chopped fresh parsley
3 tbsp chopped fresh coriander (cilantro)

Preheat the oven to 200°C/400°F/Gas mark 6. Coat the potatoes in the oil and roast in the oven until crispy. Put the whole garlic and the chillies or the pepper and chilli on the grill until almost black. Remove the skins and blend together with the mayonnaise. Season with salt and mix with the potatoes. Garnish with the parsley and coriander.

Barbecue sauce

Hot sweet-spicy barbecue sauce

1 brown onion, chopped
6 garlic cloves, finely chopped
1 tsp ground cumin
2 tbsp olive oil
50ml/2fl oz/scant ¼ cup balsamic vinegar
100g/3½oz/scant ½ cup soft brown sugar
50ml/2fl oz/scant ¼ cup Japanese soy sauce
1 tbsp Worcestershire sauce
100ml/3½fl oz/scant ½ cup ketchup
1 tbsp chilli powder

Fry the onion, garlic and cumin in oil. When the onion softens, deglaze the pan with balsamic vinegar. Add all other ingredients, boil to a sticky substance.

Elotes

Mexican grilled corn on the cob

4 fresh corn on the cobs with husk
2 tbsp butter, melted
lime wedges
200ml/7fl oz/generous ¾ cup crème fraîche
feta cheese
salt
1 tbsp chilli powder

Soak the corn in water for 15 minutes. Barbecue for 10 minutes, remove the husks, brush with butter and grill for 5 minutes more. Squeeze over lime, drizzle over crème fraîche, grate over cheese, then sprinkle with salt and chilli powder.

Apple coleslaw

Jazzed-up coleslaw with apple

juice of ½ lime
3 tbsp mayonnaise
3 tbsp olive oil
2 tbsp cider vinegar
1 tbsp poppy seeds
1 green apple
1kg/2¼lb red cabbage
salt and freshly ground black pepper

Whisk together the dressing, slice the apple into thin sticks, grate the cabbage and mix. Season with salt and pepper and leave to stand for 1 hour.

LONE STAR
LONE STAR
BEER

PART 6

DESSERTS

When it comes to Tex-Mex desserts it's almost always either one of two things: pies and paletas (homemade ice lollies). Luckily, these two also happen to be the two most delicious types of pudding you can make. In this chapter you'll learn how.

SALTY PECAN APPLE CRUMBLE PIE

This classic apple pie from Texas could very well be the ultimate crumble. The pecan nuts give crunch and a nutty flavour, whereas the salt just makes the sugar even sweeter.

SERVES 6–8

CRUMBLE
250g/9oz/generous 1 cup pecan nuts
200g/7oz/scant 1½ cups plain (all-purpose) flour
2 tbsp soft brown sugar
2 tbsp granulated sugar
½ tsp salt
½ tsp ground cinnamon
100g/3½oz/7 tbsp butter

APPLE FILLING
4–6 apples
finely grated zest from 1 lemon
100g/3½oz/½ cup granulated sugar
2 tbsp cornflour (cornstarch)
some grated nutmeg

Preheat the oven to 175°C/347°F/Gas mark 5. Bash the nuts, still in the bag, with a rolling pin or some other hard implement. Whiz in a food processor together with flour, sugars, salt, cinnamon and butter until you get a crumble.

Peel and slice the apples and mix together with the other stuff for the apple filling, then place in an ovenproof dish, about 24cm/9½in in diameter.

Sprinkle over the crumble and bake in the oven for about 40 minutes, until the crumble is crunchy and the apples soft.

Serve with vanilla ice cream, shop-bought or homemade (see p.116).

LAKELAND
PLASTICS

BOURBON PECAN PIE

Pecan pie is incredibly tasty, so tasty in fact that it can be directly life-threatening if you have a diabetic around. Pecan pie is actually also incredibly unhealthy, just butter and four kinds of sugar (and some spirits). So take a small slice and ask the diabetic to take a walk while you're eating.

SERVES 6–8

SHORTCRUST PASTRY

125g/4½oz/½ cup/1 stick butter, in cubes
250g/9oz/1¾ cups plain (all-purpose) flour
50g/2oz/scant ½ cup icing (confectioners') sugar
1 egg

FILLING

3 eggs
150g/5oz/¾ cup granulated sugar
100g/3½oz/generous ¼ cup golden syrup (dark corn syrup) or black treacle (blackstrap molasses)
1 pinch salt
1 tbsp vanilla sugar (put a couple of vanilla pods/beans into a jar of caster/superfine sugar, seal well and leave for about 2 weeks, or until it's infused with the vanilla flavour)
50g/2oz/4 tbsp butter, melted
1 tsp ground cinnamon
50ml/2fl oz/scant ¼ cup Bourbon
300g/11oz/2 cups pecan nuts, roughly chopped

Preheat the oven to 175°C/347°F/Gas mark 5. Mix together the butter, flour and icing sugar in a bowl. When you've got a crumbly substance, add the egg and 3 tablespoons water and work together to a dough. Wrap the dough in clingfilm and leave in the fridge for 20 minutes.

Press the cold dough onto a tart dish, about 24cm/9½in in diameter, and blind-bake in the oven for about 12 minutes – preferably with some rice or coins placed on top of a piece of baking parchment as a weight for a nice and neat result.

Whisk together the eggs, sugar, syrup, salt and vanilla sugar. Add the melted butter, cinnamon and Bourbon, and mix.

Place the nuts in the pastry crust, pour over the egg mixture, and bake in the oven for about 30 minutes. Keep a careful eye on the pie so that it doesn't burn; if it looks like it will, cover with foil. Take out of the oven and leave to cool.

Serve with *vanilla ice cream, shop-bought or homemade (see p.116).*

CHOCOLATE MERINGUE PIE

Merely the words 'chocolate meringue pie' will get dieticians hyperventilating and blood vessels clogging up. But scrumptious it is, and you will definitely be remembered if you serve it.

SERVES 6–8

SHORTCRUST PASTRY

125g/4½oz/½ cup/1 stick butter, in cubes
400g/14oz/scant 3 cups plain (all-purpose) flour
50g/2oz/scant ½ cup icing (confectioners') sugar
1 egg

FILLING

170g/6oz plain dark (semisweet) chocolate
100g/3½oz/7 tbsp butter
3 egg yolks
¼ tsp salt
125g/4½oz/½ cup + 2 tbsp granulated sugar

MERINGUE

3 egg whites
½ tsp salt
5 tbsp granulated sugar

Tip!

This chocolate pie can be eaten warm, cold and even frozen like an ice-lolly.

Preheat the oven to 175°C/347°F/Gas mark 5. Mix together the butter, flour and icing sugar in a bowl. When you've got a crumbly substance, add the egg and 3 tablespoons water and work together to a dough. Wrap the dough in clingfilm and leave in the fridge for 20 minutes.

Press the cold dough into a tart dish and blind-bake in the oven until cooked through for about 15 minutes – preferably with some rice or coins placed on top of a piece of baking parchment as a weight for a nice and neat result.

Prepare the chocolate filling by mixing all the ingredients together in a saucepan and then simmering for 10 minutes or until you get a thick mixture.

Whisk the meringue ingredients together until peaks form and then pour the chocolate mixture into the pastry crust, top with the meringue and chuck into the oven to bake until the meringue turns a little golden brown, about 5–10 minutes.

HELADO DE CAJETA

Cajeta, or dulce de lece, is a kind of Mexican caramel sauce that fits like a glove with homemade vanilla ice cream and toasted coconut. Despite taking a bit of cooking time, this is what I would call a foolproof recipe.

SERVES 6–8

2 large eggs
200g/7oz/1 cup granulated sugar
250ml/9fl oz/generous 1 cup milk
50ml/2fl oz/scant 1/4 cup whipping cream
1 can (400g/14oz) sweetened condensed milk
200g/7oz/scant 2 1/4 cups desiccated (dry unsweetened) coconut
salt flakes

Start by making the vanilla ice cream. Whisk the eggs until fluffy and add a little bit of the sugar at a time until it's completely dissolved. Whisk in the milk and cream and pour into an ice-cream maker. If you don't have an ice-cream maker you can, of course, use shop-bought ice cream instead.

Take the can of condensed milk and make two small holes in the lid using a hammer and nail. This is to prevent the tin exploding in your face like a delicate hand-grenade. Place it in a saucepan and fill it with water, leaving 2cm/3/4in of the can above the surface. Bring the water to the boil and leave to simmer for 3–4 hours, depending on how thick you want the caramel sauce. Top up the water if necessary.

Take the can out of the water and leave to cool for a moment. Open the can using a can opener then pour over the ready sauce into a bowl and whisk together to get rid of any lumps.

Toast the desiccated coconut. Take some ice cream and form into a snowball, roll in the coconut and drizzle over the caramel sauce. Finish off with a pinch of salt flakes.

PALETAS DE AGUA

Paletas de agua are homemade Mexican ice lollies, a bit like the ones we've got over here (but fruitier), and can come in any flavour possible. So use these as base recipes and start experimenting.

MAKES 10 ice lollies per recipe

AVOCADO
125g/4½oz/½ cup + 2 tbsp granulated sugar
2–3 avocados
2 tbsp freshly squeezed lime juice
pinch of salt

MANGO
4 ripe mangos
100g/3½oz/½ cup granulated sugar
50ml/2fl oz/scant ¼ cup freshly squeezed lime juice
cayenne pepper or chilli powder (optional)
salt (optional)

STRAWBERRY
1kg/2¼lb fresh strawberries
200g/7oz/1 cup granulated sugar
2 tbsp freshly squeezed lime juice

YOGURT AND BERRIES
150g/5oz/¾ cup granulated sugar
350g/12oz/1½ cups Greek yogurt
2 tbsp honey
400g/14oz/3¼ cups fresh raspberries, blueberries or blackberries

AVOCADO
Bring 250ml/9fl oz/generous 1 cup water and the sugar to the boil and stir until the sugar has dissolved. Leave to cool. Blend the peeled avocados, sugar syrup, lime juice and salt together to a smooth mixture.

MANGO
Blend the peeled and diced mangos, sugar and lime juice together to a smooth mixture. If you want, you can sprinkle cayenne or chilli powder and salt on this variety just before serving.

STRAWBERRIES
Mix together the strawberries and sugar and leave for 30 minutes until juicy. Simmer the mixture for 5 minutes and leave to cool. Blend with 125ml/4fl oz/½ cup water and the lime juice until smooth or leave some chunks.

YOGURT AND BERRIES
Bring 150ml/5fl oz/⅔ cup water and sugar to the boil and stir until the sugar has dissolved. Leave to cool. Blend the yogurt, sugar syrup and honey together. Add the berries.

THE POPS
Pour the mixture into an ice-cream maker and churn until you get a slush puppie. Pour into the ice pop moulds. Push down the lolly stick and leave in the freezer for at least 6 hours. You can also skip the ice-cream maker step, but the result will be icier.

Paletas de leche
RECIPE OVERLEAF

PALETAS DE LECHE

Paletas de leche are, like the name suggests, Mexican ice lollies made with dairy as the base. Keep them in the freezer and take out when you're craving something sweet, or fill a tray with ice and serve a paletas buffet for dessert.

MAKES 10 ice creams per recipe

COCONUT PALETA

200g/7oz/scant 2¼ cups desiccated (dry unsweetened) coconut
1 vanilla pod (bean)
1 can (400g/14oz) coconut milk
1 can (400g/14oz) sweetened condensed milk
200ml/7fl oz/generous ¾ cup single (light) cream
¼ salt

LIME PALETA

1 can (400g/14oz) sweetened condensed milk
50ml/2fl oz/scant ¼ cup single (light) cream
juice from 4 limes
2 tsp finely grated lime zest
salt

Dip suggestions

melted chocolate
toasted coconut
chopped pistachio nuts
crushed mini pretzels
crushed cookies

COCONUT PALETA

Toast the desiccated coconut in a dry pan until the flakes have turned a nice brown colour. Scrape the seeds out of the vanilla pod and add to the coconut milk. Add the rest of the ingredients, including the toasted coconut and stir. Pour the mixture into an ice-cream maker and churn until you get a soft-serve consistency. Pour into the ice lolly moulds, push down the lolly sticks and leave in the freezer for at least 6 hours. You can also pour the mixture straight into the moulds and skip the ice-cream maker, but the result will be a little icier.

LIME PALETA

Mix all the ingredients together and pour into an ice-cream maker and churn until you get a soft-serve consistency. Pour into ice lolly moulds, push down the lolly sticks, and leave in the freezer for at least 6 hours. You can also pour the mixture straight into the moulds and skip the ice-cream maker, but the result will be a little icier.

When the ice-cream lollies are done, just go ahead and experiment away with homemade dips and sprinkles of your choice.

SLOW BREWED
BEER
CRAFT BREWED FOR
BEER

PART 7

DRINKS

Tex-Mex drinks means, in most cases, margaritas, beer cocktails and tequila shots – all things that make you want to undress and walk out into a lake with a naked woman/man on your shoulders. But don't let that put you off, just get mixing.

Ball
MASON

MICHELADA

A michelada is a refreshing Mexican beer cocktail that's drunk either when it's very hot outside or as hair of the dog. The latter is of course not recommended. There are plenty of versions of this drink but it always contains lime, ice and chilli – sometimes tomato juice or even clamato (tomato and clam juice). Yuck. Well-cooled glasses are ideal for serving, with or without a salt rim.

MAKES 1 drink

1 lime wedge
salt
ice
330ml/11fl oz/1½ cups Mexican beer
50ml/2fl oz/scant ¼ cup freshly squeezed lime juice
½ tsp (or however much you'd like) Tabasco sauce
½ tsp Worcestershire sauce

Rub the lime wedge around the edge of a beer glass and dip it in salt.

Fill with ice and pour over beer and lime, and drip in as much Tabasco and Worcestershire sauce as you dare.

Lagerita

Since we're at mixing beer cocktails, perhaps we should try this one too? The name lets on how it tastes. Margarita + lager = Lagerita. Ingenious.

Makes 1 drink

ice
50ml/2fl oz/scant ¼ cup 100% agave tequila
1 tbsp simple syrup
juice from ½ lime
330ml/11fl oz/1½ cups Mexican lager

Fill the glass with ice. Pour in the rest of the ingredients. Drink.

1.
2.

3.
4.

MARGARITA

Even though the margarita was invented in Mexico, it's nowadays been almost completely adopted by the US where it's become something of a national drink. If you want to be more authentically Mexican, you should instead choose to mix a paloma (recipe to follow). There are thousands of variations of margarita, but here are a few of my absolute favourites.

1 Mango margarita

The perfect way to start a dinner party must be to let the guests have small talk over a table of homemade snacks and one, or a couple of deceivingly strong mango margaritas. Prepare the ingredients before the guests arrive and then stand ready by the blender to mix the drinks *à la minute*.

Makes 6 drinks

2–3 mangos
300ml/10fl oz/1¼ cups freshly squeezed lime juice
150ml/5fl oz/⅔ cup freshly squeezed lemon juice
50g/2oz/¼ cup granulated sugar
crushed ice
250ml/9fl oz/generous 1 cup 100% agave tequila
100ml/3½fl oz/scant ½ cup triple sec
salt
lime wedges

Prepare the mango purée by peeling the mangos and removing the stones. Blend until you've got a lovely purée. Pour over into a bowl. Rinse the blender and make the sweet 'n' sour mix by whizzing the lime juice, lemon juice and sugar together until the sugar dissolves. Put it in the fridge. When it's time to serve, allow 350ml/12fl oz/1½ cups ice, 100ml/3½fl oz/scant ½ cup sweet 'n' sour mix, 100ml/3½fl oz/scant ½ cup mango purée, 40ml/1½fl oz/scant 3 tablespoons tequila and 1 tablespoon triple sec per person, and mix together in the blender until frosty. Pour in a glass with salt rim and garnish with 1 lime wedge.

2 Summer margarita

You can have a lot of fun with a cucumber and some spirits. Like this summer fresh margarita with a distinct hint of melon flavour, for example. Very, very fresh.

Makes 8 drinks

150g/5oz/¾ cup granulated sugar
1 tbsp freshly squeezed lime juice
700g/1½lb cucumber, peeled and diced
350ml/12fl oz/1½ cups 100% agave tequila
250ml/9fl oz/generous 1 cup freshly squeezed lime juice
ice
salt
cucumber slies

Bring the sugar, 150ml/5fl oz/⅔ cup water and the 1 tablespoon of lime juice to the boil to turn into a simple syrup. Leave to cool. Put the cucumber, tequila and 250ml/9fl oz/generous 1 cup of the simple syrup in a blender and mix until it's as smooth as possible. Put it in the fridge. When it's drinks o'clock, pour ice into a cocktail shaker as well as 350ml/12fl oz/1½ cups of the drink mixture. Shake for 10–15 seconds and pour into a glass with a salt rim. Garnish with a slice of cucumber.

3 Hibiscus margarita

Dried hibiscus flowers from teashops, will give your margarita a lovely neon-pink colour and a tart flower taste. With what's left over from the hibiscus syrup, you can make a nice squash for the kids. You have to consider them too once in a while.

Makes 6 drinks

200g/7oz/1 cup granulated sugar
200g/7oz dried hibiscus flowers
1 lime wedge
2 tbsp ground cinnamon
2 tbsp granulated sugar
ice
300ml/10fl oz/1¼ cups 100% agave tequila
soda water
lime wedges or cinnamon sticks

Make a sweet 'n' sour mix by simmering 400ml/14fl oz/1¾ cups water, the sugar and hibiscus flowers for 30 minutes. Put it in the fridge and leave to soak for at least 2 hours or overnight. When it's time to drink cocktails, rub the lime around the edge of the glass, dip it in a cinnamon and sugar blend and fill it with some ice. Then pour in 100ml/3½fl oz/scant ½ cup of the hibiscus syrup, 50ml/2fl oz/scant ¼ cup tequila, top it up with some soda water and garnish with a lime wedge. Or if you're more fancy, a cinnamon stick.

4 Classic margarita

Tex-Mex food is all about having fun and eating and drinking colourful things with a ridiculous amount of flavour. But now and then you come across a wet blanket who complains about your mango margaritas tasting like slush puppies (yes? and?) and wants a real margarita. If so, make this one. You really can't get more classic than this.

Makes 1 drink

1 lime wedge
salt
50ml/2fl oz/scant ¼ cup 100% agave tequila, silver or gold
50ml/2fl oz/scant ¼ cup freshly squeezed lime juice
35ml/1fl oz/heaping 2 tbsp triple sec
ice

Rub the lime wedge around the glass and dip the glass in the salt. Pour the tequila – yellow or white (and the more expensive the better) – as well as the lime juice, triple sec and ice into a cocktail shaker. Shake for a few seconds and pour the strained drink into the glass.

Paloma

The national cocktail of Mexico isn't the margarita but rather the paloma – tequila with grapefruit soda. This is how to make it.

Makes 1 drink

50ml/2fl oz/scant ¼ cup 100% agave tequila
ice
freshly squeezed juice from ½ lime
grapefruit soda

Fill the glass with ice. Pour in the tequila and squeeze over the lime juice. Top up with grapefruit soda and sit yourself down to listen to the music quiz on the radio.

SANGRITA

Sangrita means something like 'little blood', and this Mex classic is just that colour (sort of). The sangrita works like a so-called chaser. You take a sip of tequila, then a sip of sangrita straight after to let the sweet-sour-hot flavour clean your taste buds so that you're immediately ready to drink some more.

MAKES 2 drinks

200ml/7fl oz/generous 3/4 cup tomato juice
100ml/3 1/2fl oz/scant 1/2 cup freshly squeezed lime juice
100ml/3 1/2fl oz/scant 1/2 cup orange juice, preferably freshly squeezed
1/2 tsp salt
Tabasco or other hot sauce
ice
80–120ml/3–4fl oz/generous 1/3–1/2 cup tequila

Mix everything together except the tequila. Serve by pouring the tequila in one glass and the sangrita in another. Drink.

Mexican sangrita

In traditional Mexican sangrita, pomegranate is often used instead of tomato juice like in the Tex-Mex variety – so you could go ahead and try that too.

Makes 2 drinks

100ml/3 1/2fl oz/scant 1/2 cup pomegranate juice
50ml/2fl oz/scant 1/4 cup freshly squeezed lime juice
100ml/3 1/2fl oz/scant 1/2 cup orange juice
Tabasco or other hot sauce
ice

Mix everything together. Drink with tequila.

MEXICAN MOJITO

Who said only Cubans can have fun and whack together mojitos? This Mexican variety of the beloved latino cocktail has a lovely bite of ginger and chilli.

MAKES 8 drinks

350g/12oz/1¾ cups granulated sugar
1 tbsp freshly squeezed lime juice
1 tbsp finely chopped ginger
½ habanero chilli
1 large bunch of fresh mint
crushed ice
400ml/14fl oz/1¾ cups tequila
350ml/12fl oz/1½ cups freshly squeezed lime juice
soda water

Bring the sugar, 350ml/12fl oz/1½ cups water and the 1 tablespoons lime juice to the boil to make a simple syrup. Add the ginger and habanero (whole) and leave to cool. Put in the fridge.

When it's time to get drunk, put 8 mint leaves in each glass, pour over 3 tablespoons of the simple syrup and muddle together (beat the sh*t out of it) with a stick. Fill the glass with ice, pour over 50ml/2fl oz/scant ¼ cup tequila and 3 tablespoons lime juice and top up with some soda water.

AGUA FRESCA

Agua fresca is a kind of Mexican non-alcoholic fruit punch that really breaks the record for thirst-quenching on a hot day. Can be made using pretty much any fruit, and if you want an extra kick, you can slip down some tequila from a hip flask when no one is watching.

SERVES 6–8

100ml/3½fl oz/scant ½ cup water
165g/5¾oz/scant 1 cup granulated sugar
½ watermelon
freshly squeezed juice of 4 limes
ice
250g/9oz/5 cups fresh mint
1 litre/1¾ pints/4 cups soda water

Make a simple syrup by bringing 100ml/3½fl oz/scant ½ cup water and the sugar to the boil. Leave to cool.

Whiz the melon in a blender, preferable without any pips, add the simple syrup and the lime juice, and pour into a large punch bowl together with ice, mint and soda water.

For the over-18s-only version, add tequila.

Agua de piña

Since pineapple is naturally acidic, this agua fresca doesn't need any lime. If you want to be a bit fancy, on the other hand, serve it out of a genuine Mexican punch bowl – a so-called 'vitrolero'.

Serves 6–8
1 fresh pineapple
250g/9oz/1¼ cups granulated sugar
ice

Mix the pineapple together with 2 litres/3½ pints/8½ cups water and the sugar in a blender. Strain to get rid of the pulp and pour into an ice-filled jug.

TEX-MEX PICKLEBACK

A pickleback is a shot of Jameson whiskey that is immediately followed by a shot of pickle juice – any kind will do. The way it works is that the sour-sweet pickle juice neutralises the alcohol flavour and quenches the gag reflex. Plus it's a bit revolting and tasty at the same time and makes you want to challenge the biggest guy/girl in the room to an arm-wrestle. In the Tex-Mex version, the Irish Jameson is replaced with some American Bourbon.

MAKES 1 shot

3–4 tbsp pickle juice, any kind will do
3–4 tbsp good Bourbon

Pour the pickle juice into a shot glass and the Bourbon in another. Then drink the whiskey first, all of it in one go you wuss, with the shot of pickle juice to follow directly afterwards.

Habanero tequila

If you want a bit more bite in your tequila, you can always flavour it with different herbs, spices and fruits. This method, however, is classic.

Makes 1 bottle

3 habanero chillies
750ml/1¼ pints/3 cups 100% agave tequila

Deseed the fresh chillies. Take a sip of tequila so that the chillies fit and then push them down into the bottle. Leave for 3 days, then strain through a sieve.

INDEX

First published in Great Britain in 2013 by
Pavilion Books
Old West London Magistrates Court
10 Southcombe Street
London, W14 0RA

An imprint of the Anova Books Company Ltd

www.anovabooks.com

Commisioning Editor: Emily Preece-Morrison
Assistant Editor: Charlotte Selby
Cover: Georgina Hewitt
Designer: Briony Hartley
Translator: Frida Green
Copy editor: Kathy Steer
Proofreader: Alyson Silverwood

ISBN: 978-1-90981-509-4

A CIP catalogue record for this book is available from the British Library.

Reproduction by Mission Productions Limited, Hong Kong
Printed and bound by CT Printing Ltd, China

First published in Sweden in 2012 as
Texmex från grunden
by Natur & Kultur, Stockholm

www.nok.se
info@nok.se

PHOTO: Roland Persson
FORM: Jonas Cramby
PROPS: Li Winther
EDITOR: Maria Nilsson
REPRO: Done